THE DARK PSYCHOLOGY

&

MANIPULATION

Know your Shadow but above all that
of others and you will live better.

II

Introduction:

Dark Psychology can be seen as the study of the human condition, in relation to the psychological nature of the different kinds of people who prey on others. The fact is that every single human being has the potential to victimize other people or other living creatures. However, due to social norms, the human conscience, and other factors, most humans tend to restrain their dark urges and to keep themselves from acting on every impulse that they have. However, there is a percentage of the population that is unable to keep their dark instincts in check, and they harm others in seemingly unimaginable ways.

What kinds of traits malicious and exploitative people have? What are the psychological drives that lead the people to act in ways that are against social norms and are harmful to others?

With The Bible of Dark Psychology & Manipulation you will learn how to understand if the people in your life harbor ill intentions against you.

You Will Learn:

What are dark Psychology Techniques Used by Mental Manipulators.

What are the Adverse Effects Dark Psychology have on People's Mind.

How People with Dark Personalities Traits Behave to Control Your Life.

How to Instantly Detect Narcissistic People and How to Effectively. Defend Yourself Against their Psychological Abuses.

How to Recognize the Manipulative People Quickly.

How to Spot Covert Emotional Manipulation in Relationships and at Work.

How Toxic People Choose their Favorite Victims.

Simple Strategies to Read Body Language Easily.

How to Defend Yourself from Deceptions Successfully.

How to Become Autonomous through Easy Steps to Take Control of Your Life.

You will learn to know and accept your Shadow but above all that of others and live better.

Dark Psychology & Manipulation provides practical actions that can create real and lasting change to help you intercept these manipulations. And how to use them to your advantage!

Even if you've never been able to defend yourself from manipulative behavior, this book will be teaching the techniques you need in your toolbox to fight all parts of Dark Psychology.

Summary

Introduction: III
   Chapter 1. How Predators Use Emotional Manipulation Tactics. 1
Emotional manipulation tactics 2
1. Get closer ... fast 4
2. Distortion of events 6
3. Raise your voice 6
4. Questions asked quickly 7
5. You are "insecure" regardless 8
6. The threat of abandonment 9
7. The projection 11
8. He will pretend total stupidity 12
9. Self victimization 13
10. suffocate yourself with love by denigrating your ex 14
11. GasLighting is one of the main emotional manipulation techniques 15
12. Denial is among the tactics of emotional manipulators 16

13. Among their techniques is intimidation .18

14. Surprises, especially bad ones, are part of the techniques...................................19

15. Personality Marketing: Another Emotional Manipulation Tactic 20

16. Humiliating sarcasm is another emotional manipulation tactic 21

17. Another tactic of emotional manipulation is triangulation...22

18. Boundary Test: One of the greatest emotional manipulation tactics 23

19. Judging others is another emotional manipulation technique 24

20. Sometimes silence can also be a tactic for emotional manipulation 26

21. Fake ignorance is among the tactics of manipulators 27

22. Domination or assertion of control is also an emotional manipulation tactic 28

23. Confusing with words 29

24. The silence..29

25. The fake good 30

26. The main symptoms...........................30

Chapter 2. Prevention strategies. 33
How to defend yourself. 33
8 ways to protect yourself......................... 39
The fog technique 46
Affective manipulation as a defense........... 55
How to fight a manipulator with a lot of practicality 59
Chapter 3 Dark side for every human being. 67
The Shadow.. 68
What is shadow?.. 69
The nature of the Shadow 70
The Shadow is projected outside 71
Representations of the Shadow: how the Shadow manifests itself 72
The paradox of the Shadow 75
Recognize the Shadow 76
What is the dark side................................. 77
Shadows 80
How to get out of the vicious circle? 82
How the Shadow manifests itself............... 83

Because it is important to recognize your own Shadow 83

The dark side is a part of us 85

DON'T BE DOMINATED BY YOUR DARK SIDE 87

KNOW THE DARK SIDE 89

HOW IT MANIFESTS 90

HOW TO DOMINATE YOUR DARK SIDE . 92

Mental manipulation: "memetics according to Dan Dennett" 93

EMPATHIC PEOPLE 95

The dark side of an empathic being 97

    Chapter 4 Deceptive personality 100

Fake people: if you know them you learn to avoid them 101

How to recognize fake people 102

How to defend yourself from bad people: but why are some like this? 114

How to defend yourself from bad people: what is useful to do 117

effective attitudes for dealing with bad people 120

Four types of fake people that are easy to spot in everyday life 127

Conclusion: 132

Chapter 1.
How Predators Use Emotional Manipulation Tactics.

Emotional manipulation tactics

Emotional manipulation tactics aren't always obvious, while physical or verbal abuse is easy to recognize because you can see or hear it.

At some point in our existence, surely we have witnessed emotional abuse or been victims of this pain. I can attest to having lived and survived this kind of abuse myself for a couple of years. Emotional abuse is hard to see often, which is why, in my opinion, it's one of the more subtle types of abuse around.

It also leaves deep scars that only truly strong individuals, who first choose the path of acceptance, then of awareness and finally that of struggle, can bring.

Emotional abuse is often planned, designed, and perfected before use, as well as being at other times a form of casual abuse used for anger or frustration.

Sounds a bit "perverse", right?

Well, in some cases it is. In other cases, it derives from a long series of abusive behaviors that span entire generations. This is why we need to recognize the tactics used by emotional abusers and manipulators to defend ourselves and put an end to these subtle attacks.

Tips on tactics used by attackers:

1. Get closer ... fast

One emotional manipulation tactic you put in place is to make you believe very quickly almost that they are in love with you or that they have a deep respect for you.

If he's not in a romantic or sexual relationship, they may try to convince you that they're your best friend after just a few days of dating.

Nice tactic, made up of many flatteries, which never tend to become offensive towards you.

Well, what happens is that they tell you some really intimate things about themselves and act like it's a well-kept secret between you two. All this aimed to build an "intimacy", if you want to call it that. So they use this intimacy to get information about you, to slowly penetrate your mind and personal sphere.

Why should this lead to manipulation?

It all seems very beautiful, spontaneous and "clean".

Here is the answer. What they tell you about themselves is almost never secret, indeed it is in the public domain, but your secrets, on the other hand, are really your personal secrets. They use these things you tell them to acquire data for manipulation, so while the things that many other people confide in you already know, yours will be well guarded and then used by the manipulator. You see ... it was a trick. They now have weapons that can potentially be used against you.

2. Distortion of events

Emotional manipulators are experts at distorting events.

If they don't lie out of habit, they will say that you are exaggerating, they will say that you said the same thing that they said, that is, that you have the same idea, even if it is not at all like that, or they will simply ignore you completely. They will lie in creative and unthinkable ways and shamelessly claim, if need be, that something happened in a way that, in reality, never happened.

Transforming facts for this type of offender is almost an art. They did it for most of their lives to get what they wanted and they got really good at it.

3. Raise your voice

Emotional manipulators scream or raise their voices, which if you're not used to this type of behavior in an argument or confrontation can be quite shocking, when there's nothing else they can use.

I apologized when I was not wrong and I apologized for the fact that he could leave. But it always took a long time to recognize what was going on.

The wisest thing that can be done is that when someone threatens to leave or acts like a capricious child, they better leave if they can't go back to civil law.

Raising one's voice is not only emotional abuse, it is also verbal abuse and one is forced to accept these situations as well.

I've seen a grown man throw a childish tantrum when caught red-handed. When he simply should have apologized for acting like a kid, instead he used the misleading and intimidating tactic of the loud voice to get what he wants ...

4. Questions asked quickly

Another very original behavior of emotional manipulators, when they want something that they know might bother you, is to ask for your opinion in a hurry.

Assuming you accept something, because you were caught off guard, they ask you questions and opinions while they are in a hurry, leave the house or run to the office, or with a short message during a work break, or even during a conversation. which focuses on other topics. Beware of this seemingly innocent tactic, which is actually emotional manipulation.

It is very subtle.

5. You are "insecure" regardless

No matter what bothers you, you have to be "insecure" regardless. This is one of the emotional manipulation tactics I've often noticed. If they have been caught flirting and you get angry, they will say that you are not sure of yourself and because of this you get angry. It seems logical to me that you are not insecure because you get angry or at least let's say that anger does not prove it conclusively.

Just because you don't want certain boundaries to be crossed by other women or men, then it's just a matter of whether or not they're boundaries in the right place, doesn't mean you're insecure in your relationship. It means you stick to your own standards and would like the other to do too. And honestly, if they don't stop using this definition, maybe it's a wake-up call not to be underestimated.

6. The threat of abandonment

An emotional manipulator will stop when he realizes he has no chance of winning an argument. Already winning, because for him arguments are a war. Their desire is that you continually seek them out and threaten to leave the relationship as well. This is especially in intimate relationships, of course.

They may not show signs of life for a few hours, all night or days, leaving you worried and nervous. Goal achieved.

It can turn out to be one of the cruelest forms of emotional manipulation. If you are caught in a moment of weakness, you will cry, seek them out and call them back over and over again trying to bring them back.

When you decide to leave relationships or friendships, you shouldn't run, shout, threaten or anything. You should act calmly "sit down" and explain that you no longer want to continue the relationship. But one should think long and hard before making this final decision.

All these performances that the manipulators make available waste a lot of time but above all a lot of energy. The next time you see them, don't be afraid and also hope it's the right time if they really leave. Nobody needs these games in their life ... believe me.

7. The projection

A manipulator uses the diversionary tactic of throwing to shift attention to another person. He never takes responsibility for his mistakes and will punctually blame someone else, which could easily be you. He projects his problem onto someone else.

He punctually removes his conscience from the weight of guilt to give it to you with joy.

The way to go is to paint yourself as dirty and laden with flaws while framing yourself. Typically, as soon as he sees a flaw,

 to scratch his own "image of perfection" immediately identifies someone to attribute it to. He will even go so far as to accuse his employer of incompetence if he fires him for his utter laziness and clearly demonstrated incapacity. His indolence, the real cause of his failure, will be completely ignored and will label the authority of inadequacy. As a couple, he will never admit his need for intimacy, make the other seem clingy and almost like he's listening attentively to your needs. He is the weak one but the tactic is based on making you look weak instead of him. While it is clear which of the two is really weak. He will repeatedly project his own self onto another subject, pointing out the mistakes, which then turn out to be his

8. He will pretend total stupidity

You will see a manipulator communicate to the world his stupidity and generalized inability. It will do this because if you put your hands forward communicating your obvious limitations when others "suffer" them, and rest assured it will happen and it will also be pointed out promptly, they can be totally relieved of their actions and responsibilities, saying: I told you so .

9. Self victimization

It will often happen that in a relationship you will put your defects and strengths on the plate, in practice yourself, you will be transparent by giving the other a vision as real as possible, making him free to make his own assessments and choices. The manipulator will evaluate them all and will probably show you that he willingly accepts you as you are and that he will respect everything about de. Later it will happen that his reaction to your legitimate way of being, obviously not really accepted by him, will be self-victimization. She will play the Oscar-winning role of the victim as soon as you try to claim your holy right to be yourself.

10. suffocate yourself with love by denigrating your ex.

Clean people don't ride the past to enjoy the present.

Denigrating a person in front of you in order to appear like a saint is a first-class emotional manipulation technique. If a relationship breaks down, it is usually the fault, if there is a fault, of both partners involved and not just one person.

As a rule, you should be cautious of a partner who degrades or knocks down their exes in front of you.

11. GasLighting is one of the main emotional manipulation techniques

To enlighten someone is to make them doubt something real that is real. Emotional and psychological manipulators use this tactic a lot. Though covertly, they ask questions that may make you think over and over again about things you've always considered sacrosanct. For example, you have just been announced as the absolute best student in your graduation class. An emotional manipulator would make you feel like it didn't happen or you were alone in the land of dreams. By acting covertly, they would make statements intended to make you feel unable to accomplish that feat. Maybe you suspect you are being used or betrayed in a relationship with them. They would ask you questions that would make you feel that the abuse is only happening in your imagination and that it is far from real. This is one of the reasons many people remain in an unhealthy relationship despite seeing the warning signs light up. Experts have suggested that in order to combat this tactic of emotional manipulation, people may need to document their experiences and life events and then constantly refer to them, so that a mischievous individual cannot even question the their existence one day.

12. Denial is among the tactics of emotional manipulators

It is difficult to separate lying, denial and distortion of facts from emotional manipulation. While a manipulator may not always be averse to the truth, their supposed acceptance serves its purpose to manipulate you later. As part of their techniques, he will accept a fact only to deny it later. This behavior is by no means an accident. He knew from the start that a problem could arise that tested their proficiency and, as such, they are quick to deny ever having a deal with you in the first place. For example, a person who has been asked to take the position of secretary at a local NGO may first accept the position, but when office requests are requested by him, he may openly deny having ever accepted that position. The same can happen in a relationship. Where emotional manipulation is what a partner has in mind, he or she would not define the relationship from the start but would continue dating the other person. As soon as a problem arises, the manipulator first denies ever having had a relationship with the victim. The idea of changing the rules while the game is still going on would leave you confused, like an unsuspecting victim. Now you begin to question yourself and blame yourself for not taking the right steps in the first place, not knowing that someone simply manipulated you.

13. Among their techniques is intimidation

In any episode of emotional manipulation, the big goal is always to control yourself. But sometimes controlling you can be difficult, so manipulators can change their systems, trying to give the world a different image of you. They attempt to achieve this by spreading untruths about you behind your back. In some cases, they may even resort to stalking, basically monitoring you. The idea is to intimidate and give people a bad impression of you. Let's say you are in a relationship with a person who uses this tactic; when you tell them that you will break up because of their bad habits, they will go around spreading lies about you. The point is that instead of knowing the true story, people would have a general dislike of you based on the falsehoods the manipulator spreads about you. You are the one seen as a bad person who broke their heart and betrayed their trust. If you aren't careful, this can even turn you against your best friends.

14. Surprises, especially bad ones, are part of the techniques

Sometimes, we want surprises from people, especially our loved ones. However, in the hands of an emotional or psychological manipulator, surprises can be employed as a tool to get you off balance. Or is it not a surprise to think that someone would keep a promise only to be told at the last moment that it won't be possible? The tactic here is to gain a psychological advantage over yourself by putting yourself in a situation where you can't help but concede to their needs. At that moment, when you probably have no other choice, they will bring out their selfish demands that you could only fulfill because of the situation. You don't usually get warned of these surprises before because, of course, it would be done in a secret, sneaky way that would make you feel like the person is trustworthy. The key to avoiding this manipulation, especially if you are a business person, is to reach a legal settlement before a deal. When a person disagrees, you must not be the victim of psychological or emotional manipulation; instead, you can easily ask for compensation.

15. Personality Marketing: Another Emotional Manipulation Tactic

This implies that someone sells you their supposed good qualities before you even know them personally. They sneak up, blow their trumpets, and advertise something good about themselves when they've sensed it's a quality you want in a partner. Let's look at it this way: Let's assume from my conversation with you I can decode that you want your partner to be someone who can swim well. As an emotional manipulator, I would start presenting myself as a swimming champion so that I can win your esteem, exploit you, and then probably dump you. This is one of the characteristics and techniques of politicians. They identify what a person likes and then pretend they own it just for the sake of what they want to achieve. Once they get their hands on what they want, you will see their true colors.

16. Humiliating sarcasm is another emotional manipulation tactic

Even if he appears to be joking, the manipulator, often sneaky, mentions the things you are struggling with in your life so that they can make you feel insecure and, in doing so, overwhelm you. They usually apply this tactic when they see that you are receiving attention or recognition that they consider superior to theirs. Can you imagine anyone joking about your exam or the failure of your marriage in public? Sure, these things are anything but funny, but they'll make them seem like some very nice clowns around.

What they really aim for is to make your immediate audience understand that you are not perfect or that you are not worth what they see in you. Perhaps you are beginning to see that some of your friends are like that; in the name of being funny, they talk about things you are struggling with in life so that they can shut you up. The way around this is to admit your weaknesses and talk about them first (where possible) before they are used against you. After all, no one is perfect.

17. Another tactic of emotional manipulation is triangulation

If you have an emotional or psychological manipulator as your partner, you are probably very familiar with this technique. It is one of the main characteristics of emotional narcissists. The idea is to validate their wrong and selfish actions towards you by resorting to a third party act. They abuse you and you react by letting them know you don't accept this behavior. However, instead of admitting their wrongs and apologizing, they direct your attention to your other friend, Vanessa, whose husband slapped her the other day and didn't protest. The idea is to make you feel like you are the only one overreacting. You will notice that they are also technically validating the abuses in this way. Triangulation is one of the defining characteristics of emotional manipulators. The principle of this emotional manipulation technique is to divert your attention by dealing with an unpleasant event from a stranger or his ex in order to justify his current wrong move with you.

18. Boundary Test: One of the greatest emotional manipulation tactics

Individuals who are manipulators don't just stick with one shot. They do what is called the "boundary test" to see how far they can cross the line. As you go along, a border crossed without retaliation would lead to crossing another and another until they penetrate your head. This is usually how attackers begin their senseless acts. They speak to you condescendingly and show "excessive understanding". Next time they will try to slap you. If it seems to them that you are capable of cashing in, the next thing you will see is that you have transformed into their punching bag. The reason for this is that at every stage they transgressed, you showed them empathy instead of resisting. Experts have said that narcissists, who are the most chronic emotional manipulators, hardly respond to empathy. What they are looking for are the consequences of their actions. So if they manage to behead you and nothing happens after that, they don't stop to think much about how she was accepted by the victim.

19. Judging others is another emotional manipulation technique

This is one of the non-hidden emotional manipulation techniques. They do it so that everyone can know and see. They deliberately implement it and you would recognize intentionality. They do nothing that is not daylight and striking. This habit of judging others is among the hallmarks of selfish and self-centered emotional manipulators. They keep pointing out your flaws and putting all your good efforts aside so that people see you as nothing but trouble. Also, this feeds their ego because, while they constantly judge you, they portray themselves as the best. One way to overcome this tactic is to detach yourself from people with this habit. Don't show them any consideration of any kind; they will not change and if you still stay with them, they will begin to affect how you live and act. You would begin to conform to shortsighted and selfish ideas and ideals.

20. Sometimes silence can also be a tactic for emotional manipulation

How do you feel when your partner is silent when you try to have a conversation with him? Chances are you'll start wondering if you've done something wrong and maybe start blaming yourself for the way you've approached them. Unnecessary silence is a means of creating confusion in you. It is also a tactic of assuming superiority and control over yourself by putting yourself on hold so that you are at their mercy. During their silence, if you haven't learned to be yourself, you may get frustrated and start asking for their attention. With this, they can manipulate you further.

21. Fake ignorance is among the tactics of manipulators

Sometimes, in an attempt to evade a task or responsibility, manipulators make you feel like you don't have the knowledge or skills to perform the task you've been assigned. This is mainly done in an organization where employee duties are not fixed. When called to do something by their boss, they pretend they have no idea of the task. The point is, you, the boss, would ultimately do the task yourself or assign it to another person. What you may not have realized from this is that they managed to control you. They tactically determine what they want to do and what not. Even children who are manipulators use this tactic to evade the tasks and chores assigned to them by their parents or teachers. Well, to overcome this manipulative tactic, try to instruct them on how to do the task and ask them to learn more about it on their own as well, instead of completely lifting them off the weight. You shouldn't give in to their petty demands.

22. Domination or assertion of control is also an emotional manipulation tactic

If you pay close attention to emotional manipulators, one of the characteristics found in all of them is the excessive desire to exert control over their victims. You will see them try to show everyone's stories by doing what they can to silence or drop perceived threats. By gaining control or dominating others, psychological manipulators hope to promote their selfish motives and keep others in perpetual bondage. When they seek dominance, they don't act covertly, but you will see them making their intentions known. Once they have achieved their goal of gaining control in a group, watch their reactions as they all become enemies of each other and retreat.

23. Confusing with words

Some manipulators are pretty good at using words. They create a web of phrases and expressions that trap and confuse the victim. They use real monologues, interrupting the other person, preventing him from expressing his opinion and managing to have control within the conversation. Alternatively, the manipulator can try to pin down words that his interlocutor has never actually uttered by trying to interpret his thinking in a distorted way.

24. The silence

When the narcissist realizes that his techniques are not having the desired effect, he can take two routes: insult or keep quiet. In the second case, the victim feels invisible and guilty. The goal is to humiliate the other person and make them feel bad for not submitting to their desires and manipulation techniques.

25. The fake good

One of the most devious manipulators is undoubtedly someone who is very friendly and good to the other person but who actually wears a mask. Although he seems capable of rejoicing with the other for the achievements, he always tries in a subtle way to instill doubt or to destroy part of the joys achieved.

26. The main symptoms

Manipulation can occur in any relationship environment, from work to friendship, and can present with a range of symptoms. According to some scholars, there are 3 levels at which symptoms could occur:

1. the first level is the level where the first signs of manipulation occur, which however could be managed with good communication. For example, there may have been states of confusion, excessive control by the partner,

people warning you about the relationship, anxiety and fear when the partner approaches, not feeling like you.

2. The second level of manipulation occurs when the person being manipulated begins to question their reasons and what they think or feel. In this phase the manipulator will begin to deconstruct the identity and self-esteem of the person with criticisms, judgments, emotional blackmail, silences, to prove that he is right and that the only point of view that matters is his. At this stage, the symptoms that trigger such manipulation in the victim are generalized anxiety, fatigue, guilt. (including things that have not been done), justification of the manipulator's attitudes, loss of interest in other things, forgetting past events or attitudes.

3. The third level of manipulation coincides with the surrender phase, where the manipulated person is totally subjugated by the manipulator who will justify him and feel deserving of the horrible treatment he is receiving. The symptoms of the person manipulated in this phase are: depression,

anxiety and panic attacks, apathy, stress, psychosomatic disorders, fear and distress.

Getting out of a period of psychological manipulation is difficult, because the main techniques are based precisely on forms of distortion of reality and annihilation of the identity and self-esteem of the person, as well as in the form of addiction. For this a long process of reconstruction and awareness of one's being and of what has happened is necessary.

As in any psychological process, the first step in improving and starting to recover is the acceptance of what has happened. To get out of this, we will then work on other processes such as the recognition of manipulative strategies, emotional reconstruction and self-respect. Following a therapy can be a help, to be able to process and overcome this moment.

Chapter 2.

Prevention strategies.

How to defend yourself.

The assumption is that the manipulator, not always aware of the techniques he adopts, will almost never decide to give up the psychological power that his techniques give him over the victim.

So the victim must first know the techniques, be aware of his emotions, listen to the body and anxiety signals, physically moving away, if possible, from the manipulator.

A true manipulator will change with extreme difficulty, in many cases never, simply because power and domination over the other are essential to maintain a winning image of oneself: a useful strategy for the victim is that, after having clear all the tactics used to clearly delineate the boundaries between oneself and the other, so as not to feel responsible for the faults and recriminations that belong only to those who commit them.

We have seen how the vampire "captures" the ideal victim with ad hoc characteristics to be able to exercise his power undisturbed. Very often, in fact, those that are clear warning signs are overwhelmed by the personality of the manipulator who questions the victim's point of view. Due to his own critical issues, he is unable to cope with the plan implemented by the vampire, ending up ignoring them, convinced himself otherwise. It is therefore essential to be able to work first of all on one's difficulties: increasing one's self-esteem, preserving one's dreams and desires, listening and validating one's emotions and needs are the first step to get out of the fog in which the manipulator relegates the victim. By starting to value yourself again, you get out of the state of confusion, going beyond the fear of seeing reality for what it really is. Recognizing that you are a victim of manipulation is the first step to get out of it, since it means taking note of playing a role in maintaining that dynamic, and therefore also of escaping it.

Remember: for fear of losing the other, we risk losing ourselves and our first right is also our first duty, to be respected and loved adequately. If we feel guilt, frustration, fear, shame ... we are not wrong, much less the emotions that, when they emerge, always have a precise meaning and an evolutionary purpose, that is to save us from what is probably the wrong situation with a person which is equally wrong.

"A state of complete physical, mental and social well-being and not the mere absence of the state of disease or infirmity". (WHO, 1948) According to the Ottawa Charter for Health Promotion, health is a resource for everyday life, not the goal of life. Health is a positive concept that values personal and social resources as well as physical abilities. Health is achieved when individuals develop and mobilize their resources in the best possible way, in order to satisfy both personal (physical and mental) and external (social and material) prerogatives. Health and disease are therefore not mutually exclusive conditions, but end points of a common continuity.

There is only one word: respect, which is the opposite of arrogance. As I said before, against all forms of violence there is only one medicine which is love.

Since the manipulator does not love, does not know or does not want to love, the love I am talking about is that towards oneself which therefore involves the recovery of esteem and trust. Never as in this case do we have to keep in mind that every day we hurt ourselves, every time we don't respect ourselves.

A fundamental step in manipulative dynamics is to gain awareness.

To do this, you may begin to tune in to yourself and your feelings, or you may start looking at yourself with compassion. Everyone has their own methods to increase the nurturing and nurturing part of themselves. Take a first step to improve your life. Then do another one.

You will only be able to change your manipulative relationship if you are willing to leave.

In many situations you will find that it is not necessary to leave. Sometimes manipulation gradually creeps into a relationship and can be eradicated. Sometimes a person only resorts to manipulation when they feel particularly insecure, so you can solve the problem by refusing to get involved and avoiding the main triggers: phrases, actions, or situations that can push you or your manipulator to tango.

Perhaps your new awareness will be enough to change the dynamics.

With some manipulators, it may be enough to reduce your engagement, without cutting all the bridges.

What will facilitate the change in the relationship is your deep commitment to achieve the life you want, a life free from manipulation.

To keep this commitment, you must be willing to do anything, even leave your love, your best friend or your perfect job behind.

You must leave his views to your manipulator, while you have your own: you must not give in to his point of view, nor try to convince him of yours.

It must be clear to both you and him that you will not accept a relationship in which you are not treated with respect and in which you will retaliate for a different point of view.

8 Ways to protect yourself.

1. Being honest with an emotional manipulator is useless. Let's imagine a situation where we honestly say "I am very sad, because you forgot our anniversary". At this point those who are good at manipulating the emotions of others will begin with an articulate and complex speech about their enormous sorrow, not failing to remind us of their critical moment, their suffering for this or that thing, their unsolvable problems - of heart, finance, business - immediately appealing to our compassion. And the hidden

message will be like "but how do you feel angry with me that I have so many problems? you should almost be ashamed ... ".

If our impression is that our interlocutor is talking nonsense - to put it mildly - then, most likely he will be!

Let's try to feel our "belly" and pay attention to the fact that those who manipulate the emotions of others, if they identify a strategy - a speech, an argument, a situation - that hooks us and makes us feel guilty, will continually use against us .

2. An emotional manipulator plays the role of the perfect rescuer very well. At any time we will be able to ask them something, the availability will always be total! Problems will arise later! Emotional blackmail At the precise moment in which we find ourselves thanking for the help received, a series of verbal and non-verbal signals will start that

aim to make us "understand" how demanding it was to help us, how hard it is to hurry to our aid, how it is difficult to always think about everything ... And it will be useless to complain that the help was offered to us spontaneously! Once again, the manipulator's counter-response will be that certain that the help was spontaneous and that only a distant, cold and unreasonable person might not notice - fantastic emotional trap: it's you who don't understand me and are not grateful. !

Two rules to overcome this situation:

when we are offered their help, empower them and clarify their commitment;

ask in advance and explicitly "can you do it for sure?

Won't it cost you too much effort? "

3. The manipulator on duty says something and then affirms, swears and swears that he never said it! His innate ability is to systematically change the cards on the table. His main skills concern the rationalization,

justification and articulated explanation of situations bordering on the absurd. Another of their outstanding abilities is linked to lying, lying in a systematic and almost pathological way. These repeated behaviors can even lead us to question reality ... Why not think about writing down everything the manipulator tells us? Why not use a pad of paper - or rather your smartphone - to write down what it tells us? His complaints? Just think that we are so distracted these days ...

4. Now let's talk about guilt. Emotional manipulators are adept at arousing feelings of guilt in others. Their ability is to make us feel guilty for saying or not saying something, for doing or not doing something, for being too much or too little emotional, for being too much or too little generous, etc. , emotional manipulators do not need to express their needs or desires, because they get them through manipulation: if they need more attention, it is enough for the "other" to feel guilty about the lack of attention ... After all we are all ready to do something to lessen our guilt. We were born with the need to be accepted and loved, and the guilt goes to

rekindle these fires. Because the emotional manipulator is a perfect victim of life, chance, others, wife, husband, children, boss, he easily inspires in others the need for care and attention. And here, right here that we must stop! Let's try to define the boundary between us and them, between their needs and our needs. Let us invite them to assume their responsibilities and free themselves from the sense of guilt: we must help those in difficulty, not those who make the difficulties of life a weapon of emotional blackmail.

"The human capacity to feel guilty is such that people can always find ways to blame themselves. (Stephen Hawking)".

5. Emotional manipulators are unfair. It is easy for them not to face unpleasant things directly, but to let others do them. The good manipulator speaks behind our backs and makes others tell us what he does not have the courage to tell us directly. They may be ready to tell you what you want to hear, just to sneakily boycott you - obviously I'm happy if you go back to working full time! Except

then, at the first opportunity, to bounce against you, in a subtle way, all the imbalances that have occurred in your family menage for your choice.

6. Let's talk a little about illnesses or physical ailments in general. If you tell the manipulator that you have toothache, he will be very willing to tell you about his dental operations or, changing the subject, his terrible back problems.

What is certain is that whatever you have, he / she will have something more serious than yours!

In this, their innate ability to attract attention in an almost compulsive way stands out. And if by chance we try to highlight their behavior, we will come across accusations of selfishness, little attention to the needs of others, little consideration of suffering not ours.

7. Emotional manipulators somehow have the ability to influence the emotional climate of those around them. When an emotional

manipulator is sad or angry, everyone around him is polluted. Probably, spreading their negative emotions allows them to feel better, more inserted and understood and, above all, more powerful and strong towards others. Spending too much time with these healthy carriers in a bad mood makes us co-dependent and entangled in a situation that easily knocks us down. And what's worse, we tend to mortify our needs and our sufferings, putting the manipulator at the center.

8. Emotional manipulators have no sense of responsibility. They are never responsible for their behavior, and it is always "someone else's fault". One of the main ways to discover a manipulator is to notice how easily they try to establish intimate bonds, entrusting us with deeply personal information in order to activate a "hook-you-so-you-pity-me" strategy. Of course, at an early stage, these people seem particularly sensitive and delicate. In reality they are far from vulnerable, and if you let them, they will latch on to you like leeches, ready to suck your lifeblood. We learn duque to recognize

these people and to keep a safe distance from them. And if we really have to stay there because close ties prevent us from escaping - parents, brothers, sisters - let's try to take them in small doses. After all, our life and well-being are the most important things we have. :)

The fog technique

It's creepy to think but ... we've all been victims of emotional manipulation at least once in our lives. Maternal pressures, feelings of guilt that lead to saying too many yes.... The even more disturbing fact is that there are people who, every day and for years, are victims of manipulators who use techniques tested and refined over time and experience.

Who is the manipulator? We don't necessarily have to associate emotional manipulation with narcissistic, antisocial, histrionic or borderline disorder, anyone can play the role of the manipulator.

A mother who uses her daughter's guilt for her own gain is also implementing a manipulation technique. Here the manipulator can be a brother, a trusted friend or a beloved mother, we are not just talking about couple relationships.

Emotional manipulation in relationships: a question of power, expectations and control

A relationship, whether it is a couple, a friendship or a parent-child relationship, should be based on mutual respect, exchange and trust.

The problem is that sometimes, a component of this relationship engages in behaviors of emotional abuse that over time become chronic and give rise to harmful consequences: worries, generalized anxiety, fear of abandonment, feelings of guilt, feelings of inadequacy, low self-esteem. .. Yes, all this can cause a single wrong relationship.

No manipulator will ever admit to being the cause of these disorders, indeed he will advise those affected to seek treatment without ever questioning themselves. The only way to defend against attacks from an emotional manipulator is to keep your distance and not be manipulated.

The parent-child relationship itself often focuses on manipulation and emotional blackmail because our educational model is based on parental authority and sees the role of the subordinate child. When family relationships are toxic, there is no clear evolution and unhealthy balances tend to be maintained; in this way, even as an adult, the child will always be seen by the parent as a "subordinate". It is truly sad to see a child who has not felt loved where he can go to redeem that love. It is crazy to watch the dysfunctional mechanisms that can be triggered in a family and it is even more terrifying to see where some couples who hurt each other in the name of love can go.

Unfortunately, manipulation is sometimes justified or even not recognized. We are living in a critical period in which, only today, we begin to shed light on the dynamics of the couple and on what is personal autonomy and emotional manipulation.

The insurmountable boundary between caring and controlling is very blurred, it can be easily seen that many of the relationships that are carried out are not based on unconditional love but on expectations, power and control. .

A relationship between two people should be born and consolidated without rigid requests, without recurring patterns and above all based on the pillars of acceptance and respect.

According to the French psychotherapist Isabelle Nazare-Aga, if it is not possible to distance oneself from one's emotional manipulator, it is possible to implement a counter-manipulation tactic that the author calls the "fog technique".

The fog technique consists of using casual, vague and almost imprecise communication, so as not to engage in verbal exchanges with the manipulator at all.

The aim is to disorient the manipulator who, no longer obtaining his nourishment (his advantage starts from the feeling of power he feels in every exchange, which he feels every time it triggers feelings of anger or despair in you) will be led to give up taking or go away.

The counter-manipulation technique aims to create distance in the bond without sending too direct signals.

The fog tactic focuses on superficial communication where the victim protects himself by answering each question in a disenchanted way, as if he were indifferent to the contents expressed by the manipulator who consequently will no longer feel important and will lose the feeling of power that is generally fueled by the manipulator. victim.

Emotional counter-manipulation can therefore be described as a one-way communication in which the manipulator sends messages / provocations / criticisms / accusations and the victim responds without aggression and vehemence, slipping every manipulative attempt, every accusation or word on him.

In this way, the interlocutor (the victim) will not take the blows but will put in place a passive resistance capable of causing a spontaneous removal of the manipulator.

Very often victims of emotional manipulation tend to initiate a tug-of-war with the manipulator - nothing more wrong! The fights, the challenges, the competitions, the progress and the setbacks, are all dynamics that feed the lust of the manipulator. If an arm wrestling instigates, the fog technique disengages in a subtle and intelligent way.

The fog technique is easier to describe than to implement. In the dialogue with the manipulator (when he plays the role of a mother or an ex-husband with whom you share the children) there is a strong emotional charge. The interlocutor will have to learn to weigh each word well and to measure the information provided.

Communication with the manipulator, when the interlocutor has no control and awareness, is nothing more than a labyrinthine path where it is the manipulator who sows confusion and uncertainty. Here the victim's task is to overturn this scenario and do it on tiptoe, without being caught in the act.

To successfully implement the fog technique, I recommend that you:

Give the manipulator as little information about your life as possible by using vague communication.

Here is a practical example.

Manipulator: "How did the job interview / appointment go?"

Victim: "I don't know, I don't want to pronounce myself ... this time I want to be superstitious".

Mitigate your reactions. Manipulators are famous for reviving stories or inventing facts out of thin air. If he gives you sensational news, mitigate your reactions and always check the facts without starting in fourth grade. Here is a practical example.

Manipulator: "Do you know that Sara has a lover?" or "Professors criticized your child's education"

Victim: "How strange, I never would have said".

Don't flatter yourself too much if she starts complimenting you or making sudden expressions of love, love bombing is a very effective and very dangerous emotional manipulation technique. Flattery, compliments, and those attitudes that make you feel important can only mean that the manipulator wants to tighten his grip on you.

Check your emotions and pay attention to the tone of voice you use, as well as your appearance or facial expressions.

Minimize his accusations without taking offense. This is difficult to do. If the manipulator accuses you of being unfaithful, superficial, stupid ... pretend to be surprised by his reaction and minimize your behavior that is the object of criticism by truncating the subject soon.

If you are cornered, they suggest you adopt a healthy and protective "no contact". "No contact" creates distances in a less indiscreet way but allows you to recreate and reorganize your life based on what is really important for your well-being.

If he asks you a vague question, be confused and ask the manipulator to clarify what he means.

If you want to resist an emotional manipulator, in addition to the fog technique, there is one more thing you can do: work on your self-esteem and your inner working core. Basically, recognize your worth and work to identify what your goals and needs are.

Those who become prey to an emotional manipulator, in general, need to receive the approval of others for their choices or find themselves trying without giving space and voice to their real needs.

I do not want to generalize but ... it is true, often the victims of manipulators are people who do not have much confidence in themselves and always adapt to the conditions imposed by the other without respecting or validating their own needs ... indeed, waiting for somebody miraculously arrives to recognize them and maybe please them.

Unfortunately I tell you that if you don't roll up your sleeves, no one will come to meet your needs and heal your deepest wounds. In engaging in the emotional counter-manipulation technique, always remember that loving each other is a fundamental pillar for moving functionally between one relationship and another and within life itself.

Affective manipulation as a defense

By skillfully using the lie, the manipulator configures situations in his perspective to confuse his victim. The manipulator uses human relationships to his advantage, relying on very subtle psychological and affective mechanisms and totally destroying those who come into contact with this perverse mechanism. An affective manipulator destroys self-esteem and subdues his victim, who sometimes cries and despairs without even understanding why. Carries out some behaviors with manipulative intentions, such as the treatment of silence with the aim of frightening and subduing the manipulated subject. In some cases, an affective manipulator is able to emotionally subdue a person even without necessarily having low self-esteem and therefore should know how to defend himself. The direct line that is established between the victim and the perpetrator of the crime provokes in the victim a constant need for approval by the latter, a continuous need for consent from the manipulator, to the point of becoming dependent on it in an uncontrolled way. He requires the victim's attention and understanding but is unwilling to do the same.

Many times an affective manipulator presents himself as a helpful, very rich and charming person. They are very adept at hiding their way of being by making it difficult to defend themselves. They are usually very intelligent and cultured people, generally non-violent and very devious, as well as difficult to identify. The manipulator transforms reality trying to deconstruct the human and sensitive part of the victim and making it incredibly fragile and susceptible, exploiting its weak points and abusing them in every way.

To react, it's important to start by not justifying ambiguous behavior, very dubious excuses, or continuous promises. Faced with these attitudes, it is advisable to shut up and interrupt the conversation as soon as possible. It is also important to break long-standing habits and not answer ambiguously phrased questions. Asking for help from a therapist and talking about it with other people, perhaps participating in help groups to defend themselves from narcissistic manipulators and dealing with other people who have experienced the same experience are the first steps to take for those who need to free themselves from emotional addiction.

Reborn after emotional manipulation

Many times a "manipulated" experiences feelings of resentment and anger that could lead him to emulate some behavior of the affective manipulator. The most common feeling after the story is over is that of a sense of strangeness and deep disappointment. He feels he has wasted his time and trust in him and feels disillusioned and deeply sad.

In this case it is important to understand that nothing was done wrong, that one's intentions had a positive purpose and that they are a beautiful part of one's being to be preserved and positively valued. It will therefore be necessary to understand that we need to rebuild a life and put this parenthesis aside by learning from our mistakes. Stop suffering and understand your worth, which does not require someone else's need and validation, but which is a feeling that must come from yourself.

If a person learns to love himself and to discover his own worth, he will hardly fall victim to a manipulator again, since he will not need anyone's confirmation to be aware of his reality as a loved and desired creature.

How to fight a manipulator with a lot of practicality

Below I summarize five strategies for successfully defending yourself from manipulators and which will also contribute to personal growth and the maintenance of an adequate psychological balance.

Express what you disapprove of and how you feel

One of the manipulation techniques focuses on criticism. When we criticize a person's behaviors, attitudes, decisions and skills ..., they usually feel less confident and are more likely to accept the manipulator's needs. In other cases, the person adopts a defensive, almost aggressive attitude, I would say aimed at opposing all the arguments that annoy him. In the first case the manipulation takes place starting from the management of our self-esteem, in the second case starting from the control of our emotions. In one form or another, we remain at the mercy of the manipulator.

What to do?

Express your ideas clearly and simply. It is essential that the other person realizes that they will not be able to influence our judgment or reflexive ability by manipulating our self-esteem or our emotions. Aggressively opposing the arguments of the other, which many times have no solid foundation, would only lead to useless discussions and the impossibility of understanding each other.

We must always keep in mind that our goal is not simply "not to let him manipulate us for any reason", but to change the situation. Why this goal? Because surely the person who will try to manipulate us is an important person for us and we will therefore be interested in reaching a profitable agreement, both to maintain a good personal relationship and to develop a business together. Therefore, it is essential that our message is not only understandable but also that it is received by our interlocutor with as little resistance as possible.

Let us also remember that expressing how we feel about something or someone is a very effective technique, as long as it is implemented correctly and respecting the other. When our interlocutor listens to us talking about our moods, he will have the perception that communication flows, is open and sincere. Also, we will "force" him to put himself in our shoes, to be empathetic with what we feel, so he will likely reflect on the effects of his manipulative behavior.

Express yourself!

On many occasions the manipulator takes the conversation to no man's land, makes criticisms without personalizing, from a position without compromise; always leaving an escape route in case someone asks him who he refers to.

The best defense against this communication strategy is to personalize, personalize, personalize ... he Always speaks in first person and ask for clarification. An example would be: "I hear you refer to ... is that so?" "Forcing" him to take responsibility for his judgment normally disarms the manipulator and blocks his strategy.

Limit your responsibilities and accept your mistakes

Another of the manipulative techniques par excellence is to make the person feel guilty, making them feel responsible for everything that has happened, what happens and what will happen.

Sometimes we have a certain share of responsibility but our share of "guilt" is not infinite. A very effective strategy is to delimit our responsibilities and recognize our mistakes. We have the right to make mistakes but no one has the right to take advantage of it and tear our self-esteem apart because we were wrong.

Recognizing our difficulties and our share of responsibility indicates that we are mature people, responsible for our actions and therefore not very manipulable.

However, the question remains: how to put the previous three points into practice?

Express yourself with firmness, serenity and confidence

We have already said that one of the manipulator's favorite weapons is to play with emotions. This is why it is essential to establish dialogue from a position of trust, firm and serene.

We must always keep in mind that the manipulator is not interested in initiating a constructive debate but only in achieving his goals, for this reason if we offer him logical arguments that contradict his ideas, he will probably take our opinions and reuse them according to his interests. . We always remember that even the best idea can be seen in a different perspective and the manipulator is very skilled in playing with the different possibilities.

So what do you do?

Recognize that his ideas are valid, don't criticize them, rather use phrases like: "I understand your point of view and respect it; even if I believe that ... "or:" your point of view is adequate; but even so there is always the possibility that… "In this way a model is inserted into the conversation: respecting the opinions of others, valuing his ideas, we will also give value to our own.

Neurolinguistic programming (NLP) experts also recommend replacing the annoying "but ..." with words like: anyway, and despite ... they are less harsh and are better accepted.

Adopting this strategy, even if not completely infallible, will undoubtedly help us to control our emotions and offer a more serene image of ourselves.

Feel free to deny yourself!

If we have a solid and sufficient basis against the idea that is proposed to us, then ... denying oneself will not be a sin. However, we shouldn't get lost in trivial excuses or self-blaming explanations. Expressing our disagreement is a right that allows us to establish our limits and highlight them in front of the people around us.

Accepting other people's requests to avoid an argument often involves giving up a part of our individuality and giving in to manipulation. So be consistent and say "No" as often as necessary.

Deciding to fight a manipulator does not lead us to an easy path to follow, we will encounter many obstacles. Many times this implies giving up the comfortable positions we have assumed for the duration of our life, both in the family and at work, but it will undoubtedly allow us to be more consistent with ourselves and will facilitate the identification of the path to find our balance. emotional.

Chapter 3.

Dark side for every human being.

The Shadow

Sometimes we happen to be unaware of what is happening around us, to be the root cause of our suffering or that of others without being able to admit it. Here we are talking about the Shadow, the most unconscious part of us, the one that hides from the conscience to hide the most negative part from the conscious part.

Basically, people connect their Shadow side to all those negative aspects, to those images of themselves to repudiate, condemn and then hide.

of this he has dealt with literature with Dr. Jekyll and Mr. Hyde, and cinema, for example with Fight Club, tales of how the relationship with his shadow can be conflicting if not tragic.

What is shadow?

The Shadow is a concept that Jung formulated to describe the set of undeveloped functions and attitudes of the human personality, it represents all the rejected, removed and unauthorized contents from consciousness, for the education and influences to which the individual is subjected

With many names, psychology has tried to define the dark side of our personality: depression, anxiety, narcissism, manipulation, victimhood ..... Shadow is a psychic content that is not related to consciousness, or at least of which one is little aware. Shadow is what a person believes he is and does not want to be, the sum of all the unpleasant qualities you want to reject, the dark side in us or what you consider unacceptable.

The Person is, for Jung, understood according to the ancient meaning attributed by the Greeks, that is the mask that each of us wears and that is determined by the role he occupies within society. But as the outside exists there is the inside: the Shadow contrasts with the Person, that is, the unconscious, which establishes a compensatory relationship with it, like good and evil.

The nature of the Shadow

Carl Gustav Jung believes that the human being delegates to the Shadow everything that he believes to be negative: the Shadow becomes the weight of all human feelings that generate sense of guilt, shame, pain, perversion and whatever else the Superego may deem worthy of being judged and excluded. To really know who one is, says Jung, one must start by recognizing that the

Shadow also exists in itself and that all the darkness that we recognize around us actually lives inside us first.

The Shadow is projected outside

The Shadow, like everything unconscious, is projected. What does it mean? It means seeing in others the aspects and qualities of which we are not aware, and therefore, we feel particularly attracted to the people we project on. Consequently, we do nothing but think about them, observe them and talk about them, as if they were the center of our attention.

Maybe we think about that person "What an untrustworthy person! I can not stand her!" and then we do not want to recognize something similar to our character. In summary, the deep unjustified antipathies are almost always the result of the projection of one's own Shadow.

Representations of the Shadow: how the Shadow manifests itself

The Shadow manifests itself in various dominant negative attitudes. There is the Shadow represented by those people who usually blame others for their incapacity: the others are responsible for their unhappiness and by virtue of this 'injustice', they demand some sort of compensation for the wrongs suffered.

When our life is dominated by this type of Shadow, it may happen that, not understanding the reasons, they become hostile with everyone (and the first targets are, paradoxically, those who try to help them), hurting themselves and / or to the others.

In such cases you can get into depression, have attitudes like: "... I'm sick, I can't, everyone against me, I don't feel like it, don't expect anything from me, etc.".

Another figure is that of the 'unscrupulous', of 'the end justifies the means'; in this case, the superego is condemned to exile with the ephemeral result of having the feeling of being free from any moral, ethical or common good concern. What matters is to aim for the purpose, to bring home the result, overcoming if not even removing any pre-existing moral principle.

In this climate, one is exaggeratedly alert and everything that is seen as not useful is branded as harmful and any subjects who set out on their own 'path' are perceived as a threat or a challenge to be faced and overcome.

How many friends, relatives, partners, etc, (or us) do they make us aware of their incurable suffering and in doing so make the other feel guilty? In doing so, those who are dominated by this Shadow behave in a blackmailing manner for the sole purpose of dominating or suffocating others.

Then we cannot fail to mention those who in order to reach an impossible perfection, that is, to be at the height of an impossible goal, continually try to improve themselves, taking endless courses, without however ever feeling ready to commit to something to achieve.

On the other hand, there are subjects who have destructive behaviors and with possible addictions (drugs, alcohol, drugs, games, shopping, etc.) Such people preclude any possibility of relating, have a non-existent self-esteem, difficulties in the working world and are prone to a very often uncontrolled use of physical and psychological violence. Their inability to control themselves often leads them to commit criminal acts.

Other manifestations of the shadow are those represented by inveterate seducers, by those who are pathologically addicted to love and sex, by those who go crazy when they think they are in love and then feel destroyed when it ends; those who identify with work and make it their only reason for living; people who use authority to crush others or who are very skilled in declining all that is positive to the negative (of themselves and of others).

The paradox of the Shadow

According to Jung, the man who identifies with his public image by neglecting his unconscious life causes this part he has ignored to come out on its own, with explosive force, in the relationships he has with the people around him.

Therefore, the more we tend to keep the Shadow in an unconscious dimension, the more it grows, expands, becomes voracious and acquires power. The shadow, if it remains isolated from the totality, progressively leads to a deconstruction of the Person and feeds in the human being such a destructiveness as to boycott and ruin himself and his relationships: the world is increasingly beginning to be looked at and interpreted through lenses. altered and sick that distort its shape and lead it, more and more, to deconstruction and annihilation.

Recognize the Shadow

The way forward is therefore to pay attention to this inner personality, literally speaking to oneself. You should overcome any embarrassment in doing so and allow each part of yourself to talk to the other, so that both can feel fully heard.

It is important to maintain a non-judgmental attitude. If you judge the other part of yourself, it could gain power because it feels offended and therefore justified in its complaints. This is where therapy can help. "The course of therapy is therefore like a conversation with the unconscious," writes Jung. And when they feel heard, the tensions between the internal and external personality subside, giving a more serene life. Also, you will have more energy to face life, because you will feel less at war with yourself and the people around you.

What is the dark side

What is the dark side, how does it affect our life and how to get rid of it? Remember "The Strange Case of Dr. Jekyll and Mr. Hyde"? By day Jekyll is a respectable doctor, by night a monster capable of any atrocity. Here, Mister Hyde, as it were, is our shadow (dark side), or his physical manifestation. Carl Gustav Jung, the famous Swiss psychoanalyst, in particular addressed the subject in an exhaustive way, but Peppa Pig also, in a small way, speaks about it in the language of her children. Just think of the episode entitled "Shadows" in which Peppa and her friends try to sow them by running fast. Little Rebecca Rabbit and Mr. Elephant admonish: "No one can escape his shadow George". And the little elephant specifies: "When something is between the Earth and the Sun, it casts a shadow". Childish wisdom!

Because this is exactly what happens with the shadow, even the inner one: we cannot get rid of it, but if we want, it is possible to integrate it into ourselves, or to accept it, without running the risk of projecting it onto someone else, be it the partner, friends, parents and anyone they meet in their path. Having said that, let's find out what the shadow, or dark side, is, according to Jungian theories. Obviously they are not intended as absolute truths but they can certainly represent an interesting point of view on the insidious topic.

The individual shadow, as Jung understands it, is a component of the personality, the repressed side, "the dark brother", or all those "defects" (or presumed such) that we do not admit we have because they are unacceptable in the light of conscience. The personal shadow is the result of everything we have included in the course of our growth path due to the ethical-moral constraints due to the training environment. To give a concrete example, let's think of a greedy man who does not recognize this negative characteristic and who, therefore, projects greed onto others. Not recognizing his greed, he negatively judges the greedy, which he often encounters on his path.

Usually we are not at all aware of this mechanism, we are victims of it and as such we continue to live as if the guilt, the evil, the negativity belonged to others rather than to ourselves. If we only began to reflect in these terms, we would gradually realize that what we hate most corresponds exactly to our dark sides, removed from consciousness. For example, those who are sure they are not arrogant but often identify this defect in those around them, are most likely a victim of this mechanism. Therefore, within himself, he hides arrogance.

Shadows

While Jung identifies the individual shadow, as illustrated in the previous paragraph, on the other hand he believes that there is also a collective shadow. The latter is linked to the universe of archetypes, or rather to the innate and predetermined ideas of the human unconscious. In fact, Jung was convinced that the unconscious of each of us, from birth, contained innate, primordial, collective mental images, in the sense that they belong to everyone, regardless of personal formation. The whole of these archetypes would form the collective unconscious.

Jung identifies several but I limit myself to mentioning two, the Animus, that is the male archetype that resides in the female unconscious, and the Anima, the female archetype that resides in the male unconscious. What does it mean? That in each of us, regardless of the gender we belong to, a male and a female part coexist, often not in balance with each other. For example, it happens that in women the male part is repressed and in the same way that men repress the female part.

What happens if the two sides are unbalanced? We project on the partner, but also on friends and acquaintances, the non-manifest part. If, for example, I am very feminine and I reject my more aggressive masculine side, I will tend to look for a man who compensates for my lack, therefore tendentially aggressive. This mechanism leads us to choose partners of a certain type, perhaps always the same, to compensate for the characteristics that we would like to integrate into ourselves.

How to get out of the vicious circle?

According to Jung we should recognize the missing archetype and try to integrate it within ourselves. This is the case of an impractical woman who always couples with authoritarian, practical and strict partners. A choice that could be motivated by her unconscious desire to integrate within herself the qualities embodied by that kind of man, therefore greater severity, practicality, authority.

How the Shadow manifests itself

The individual shadow mainly manifests itself through the above dreams and projections. In the dream world it often takes the form of a figure of the same sex as the dreamer or an animal, which behaves very differently from the dreamer himself. Its purpose, in fact, is to integrate, compensate, the qualities that the dreamer does not dare to manifest in his conscious life. Projections, as we have already seen, instead consist in attributing our worst defects to someone else, without realizing it.

Because it is important to recognize your own Shadow

Those who are victims of the Shadow, or those who are not aware of it, tend to blame others because of the projection mechanism.

Understanding it helps to get out of this logic and to understand that the defects of others, especially those that bother us most, actually belong to our interiority. It is certainly not an easy job, also because the conscience, until it gets used to it, tends to deny the obvious. But you can always learn: it would be enough to start doing it in everyday life!

When a defect of others particularly disturbs us, we should look within and try to understand if in some dark cave of our soul the same defect is hidden and cleverly disguised. Once we have become aware of it, we can finally turn it into a constructive "defect". Let us take the example of a greedy man who at some point realizes he is. By becoming aware of this, his greed can gradually turn into thrift, that is, the bright face of greed. Why isn't darkness necessarily bad? Because it depends on the use we make of it. Furthermore, becoming aware of one's shadows certainly improves relationships with the outside world because it helps us to see others for what they really are, for the benefit of altruism and sincere sharing. Obviously it is a complex process, which most of the time requires the support of professionals, in order to avoid making gross mistakes.

The dark side is a part of us

There is the dark side in the human soul, an incomprehensible part that can even be scary.

Sometimes it happens to feel emotions that bring out a negative part of us that perhaps would never have come out.

This path can manifest itself in various forms, starting from small common signs such as a recurrent bad mood up to even the most absolute self-harm, ranging from severe eating disorders to suicide. This is because, paradoxically, the dark side pushes us to seek emotional fulfillment in pain that we cannot find anywhere else.

Have you ever noticed? When we are very sad, in the throes of negative emotions, we tend to accentuate this mood by listening to melancholy music, watching sad movies, stopping eating or overeating. Probably in an attempt to make our inner pain physical and plausible.

When we are unhappy, our negative side prompts us to try to suffer even more.

Of course, rationally, nobody likes their unhappiness. In fact, unconsciously, we are looking for a form of participation in our pain or a feeling of deep empathy with those we feel is natural and necessary to have it.

But it is not easy to manage the dark side of our soul without awareness of what is happening inside us. All of this, in fact, can easily turn into an uncontrolled river of emotions. With its current, this river drags us away making us unreachable even to those who sincerely want to help us.

It is vital to realize that the dark side is a part of us as well as our best side. We cannot expect someone else to notice our malaise and take charge of it. We are simply able to resist that current only by deciding to get out of it.

The human soul is a great mystery and nothing can really make us imagine how deep and intricate it can be. It's easy to get lost without following the light of common sense.

When negativity takes hold of our heart, let us remember that we always have the power to decide which direction to move our emotions. Our best part is always at hand

DON'T BE DOMINATED BY YOUR DARK SIDE

THE "DARK SIDE", WHAT JUNG DEFINES SHADOW, IS A SIGNIFICANT AND WELL-GROWN PART IN ALL OF US: ACCEPTING THIS REALITY IS THE FIRST STEP TO UNDERSTAND IT.

Knowing oneself means exploring the darkness, deepening and making contact with everything that we refuse to see, because it is submerged below consciousness, but which can be deduced by shedding light on our fears, on the annoyances we feel, on what we tend to avoid, negative emotions, destructive thoughts.

Accepting the fact that we cannot eliminate this dark side but only control it is essential for not being dominated by it. So let's find out what it is and how to live with it.

KNOW THE DARK SIDE

But how is the Shadow born? Psychic contents, the awareness of which would be intolerable, are masked and removed, but they continue to operate from within. Here lurk the frustrated desires, traumas, negative experiences, delusions, limitations and conditionings sewn on our true being, which lead to the development of certain behaviors and personality characteristics; it is the emotions, the desires, the behaviors that we hate, of which we are ashamed, aspects of us that create discomfort and that we judge negatively, even when, in fact, they are not.

In the same way, the potentialities contained within us, but which we are not able to develop, are also part of the dark side: recognizing that others have obtained what we would like, can generate in us antipathy or an unhealthy adoration for these people, a according to the projected internal need.

All that we reject about ourselves does not just remain under the surface, but creates an internal pressure that can be partially released, using the mechanism of projection. Since the shadow is experienced as unacceptable, it must be attributed to others, in fact by removing it it is possible to control it and make it harmless. As a result, we never see others for what they really are, but we can indirectly observe who we are and how our unspeakable desires reveal themselves.

HOW IT MANIFESTS

The unmet needs that fuel the dark side are pressing to be met, and the paths they take to get the energy needed are subtle and camouflaged.

Typical manifestations are:

- complaints, depression, victimization behaviors, incessant protest against the injustices suffered;

- the sense of guilt, poured out on ourselves or on others, to which the cause of one's failures is attributed;

- the need to be stunned, to escape, from addictions to avoid the pain of loneliness;

- hostility towards others, judgment, criticism, suspicion, revenge, resentment;

- pursue their own goals without moral scruples, thirst for power and success, psychological manipulations;

- set unrealistic expectations and waste time and energy chasing illusions;

- continue to flee from their fears and avoid situations, remaining immobile;

- envy, flattery;

- excessively admire someone, idealize them to compensate for their deficiency;

HOW TO DOMINATE YOUR DARK SIDE

The polarity of the shadow is part of the personality of each of us, it is invisible but inseparable from who we are. The goal, therefore, is not to eliminate it, purify it or more effectively try to repress it, but to integrate it in its entirety. Knowing what is hidden allows you to master it.

In this way negative energy can be transformed into a resource and a guide for our actions, without being overwhelmed by it. We simply have to start observing ourselves, without making judgments, but accepting what we are: we analyze the emotions we feel, the behaviors and reactions we have towards others, especially in stressful situations, when the responses are not mediated by the filter. of consciousness.

Governing the dark side requires constant attention and patient work on oneself to reinvest energy, removing it from all that is destructive or self-destructive (criticism, hostility, complaining, addictions, etc.) and directing it towards creative occupations, which they allow self-realization and evolution.

By knowing our projections, we can rediscover the power to choose and the responsibility to act, no longer blaming the outside or finding flaws in it, so as not to face the scariest part of ourselves.

Mental manipulation: "memetics according to Dan Dennett"

Do you know what a meme is? it is an idea, a concept, a belief that is passed on from one person to another. These beliefs have the same properties that viruses and bacteria possess: contagion by contact, rapid expansion, self-propagation and above all they are harmful. This term was coined by scientist Richard Dawkins and made known in his book "The Selfish Gene" ... Is "mental manipulation" one of the closest topics to memetics?

Dennett, who I believe is one of the leading thinkers of our time, exposes beautifully what memes are and above all what memetics are. People often say to me "hey but why are you studying these things? Aren't they the dark side of psychology? "sure! that's why we have to study them.

I really like the parallel he draws between the infections we carry and that we have brought to other cultures - with the most striking example of Europeans bringing viruses to the Americas and exterminating entire populations - with the export of memes to societies that don't. still have. It is clear that here we could do a lot of sociology and politics talking about healthy bearers of "democracy" ... but this is not the exact place to do it.

Another very beautiful intuition, typical of Dennett, is that of applying evolutionary thinking to human thought. Indeed, Dennett says: "It is not clear why there is no doubt that the webs a spider creates are the work of evolution while there is doubt that the web is an evolutionary operation." The crux of the matter for me lies in personal development and concerns the famous systemic maxim "the actions that man does are always the best choice for himself in that particular moment". This means that all works of human thought, however horrible they may seem, are always aimed at evolution.

Studying memetics to find out how we are manipulated or how, simply, some ideas can be harmful, I think it's a more than noble purpose. And I strongly believe that even read-only is a great antivirus ☺

EMPATHIC PEOPLE

Empaths are generally known as the healers of the world.

They are people whose senses are heightened and amplified, they are individuals who not only see and feel the different energies of the world, but who actually experience them on themselves.

Those who are not empaths may think that this ability to feel what others are feeling is a gift, but if you can persuade an empath to tell us about their 'gift', they may confide in us that it is not always a starry sky. Even if he is aware that he has an important quality, he may confess that it is a burden, often almost unbearable.

Many people rely on them for support and understanding. Empaths almost always win the trust of others, because they make people feel safe. And while the empath is able to manage the emotions of others, at the same time he experiences them on himself and all of this can lead to stress and emotional breakdowns.

The dark side of an empathic being

The dark side of an empathic being comes in the form of two contrasting voices, which speak to him almost constantly in his head.

He can constantly feel good and bad, negative and positive, to the point of being overwhelmed by them, in case he is unbalanced and well shielded from what he attracts.

Empaths are more sensitive to the negative energies of life.

Their intense ability to feel cannot escape the deep evils that exist in the world. Their deep understanding of what exists and operates in the world is enough to confuse and sadden them. For this very often they tend to be melancholy, the emotion that dominates them, in fact, is sadness.

The dark side of an empathic individual is constantly being exhausted and fatigued by the energies that are absorbed. Despite this, he is able to silently observe, recognize and hear.

Empaths want to be loved just like all other people and accepted for who they are. But it is their generosity and kindness that often leads them to be exploited by those who only want to take and never give. Empaths are "givers" and receivers, ready to show kindness to those who need it most at any time.

The dark side of being empathic is that it often takes a back seat for the sake of others. An abandonment that is built over the years, until the consequent need to go in search of one's soul, once again, a need that arises only when one feels completely lost.

This is why the empathic person always keeps a small part of himself away from the rest of the world. Maintain some sort of defensive barrier out of necessity.

The dark side of being an empath is the war he has always lived within himself. The war he wages against sadness and darkness, which tries to raise his repulsive head to lead him to self-destruction.

The only way to combat all this is to know how to distinguish between authentic emotions and false emotional energies, which invade it from the outside. Empaths need people who can understand who they are and what they live.

They need to be able to lower the wall they have built around them and learn to express the feelings they have, so that this precious gift can do good in their life as well.

If not, empaths are bound to fight a war within themselves, which will never end.

Chapter 4.
Deceptive personality.

Fake people: if you know them you learn to avoid them

Do you know how to recognize fake people? Here are some tips to permanently remove them from your life and improve it.

Sooner or later in life we have all had to deal with fake people: a friend or a friend with ambiguous behavior, someone whose thoughts and feelings were never really clear or, worse, in the end they turned out to be the exact opposite. of what emerged on the surface.

When the mask falls and we discover the true face of what we believed to be a friend, who will therefore fall by right into the category of false people, the disappointment and the sense of betrayal can be great, especially if we had invested a lot in that relationship and believed in friendship that bound us to that certain person.

And then, how to recognize a person's falseness before it is too late? Paying attention to these five signs could help you.

How to recognize fake people

1. Evaluate the time the person devotes to you. If she needs a ride, you're the first person she calls, and if you have a party invite you can't miss, she convinces you to take her with you. But when you ask for a favor or simply because you are feeling down and want the comfort of a friendly voice, there is no cell phone, the cell phone does not respond, you have a fever, you have a work commitment that cannot leave.

2. Notice how he talks about other people. «Francesca is a dead cat. Andrea is a

parasite. Luca is cheating on Marina with his sister's friend, but on the other hand Marina has married him out of interest, so it suits her». And so on.

If this person whom you think your friend talks about others in this way, one wonders how they will talk about you, right? If his tongue can be so ruthless and cutting, rest assured that sooner or later he will cut you too, just turn your back. Whoever always has a "good" word for everyone, will one day have it for you too.

3. Give credit to your "gut" feelings. It happens that when you are together, for some reason that you can't even explain to yourself, you never feel completely yourself and you can't really be relaxed. You have a feeling of subtle discomfort, of annoying discomfort, something tells you that it is better not to open completely. That something is your instinct, and it's usually not wrong - maybe you better listen to it.

4. Lies, envy, competition. Not infrequently, false people are false because they feel insecure and have an inferiority complex and inadequacy with respect to everything and everyone. This leads them to lie often, to tell unlikely feats of which they are unlikely protagonists, to compete with others on anything and to show envy for those who are richer, smarter, have more hair, hook more. If you let him think he's the best, you'll make him harmless.

5. Observe how he reacts to your successes. He says «Brava! Congratulations! "But his lips twitch into a grimace that looks more like a grin than a smile. Maybe your friend isn't inwardly happy with your promotion.

Aphorisms about fake people

Perhaps as a compass you can also use these sayings and aphorisms about hypocrisy which are basically phrases against fake people:

Not talking about oneself at all is a distinct hypocrisy.

The hypocrite, therefore, does not say what he thinks because he does not want to be judged: the hypocrite therefore denies himself because he does not intend to confront the reality that surrounds him, because he does not want to oppose an opinion that enjoys credit in the world .

False indignation is the most repugnant form of hypocrisy.

The hypocrite does not want his thought to be captured, so he cleverly and completely hides it.

I wonder if there is more sin in following what I feel or in the hypocrisy of living what I am not.

The most difficult and exhausting of all vices, hypocrisy is a round-the-clock task.

The hypocrite constantly strives to look good, even if it is bad.

The only vice that cannot be forgiven is hypocrisy. The repentance of a hypocrite is itself hypocrisy.

Hypocrites are rogues in the guise of saints.

No one can have one face for himself and another for the crowd for a long time without risking not knowing which is the real one.

Hypocrisy is not the hypocrite's tool, but his prison.

The humility of the hypocrite is pride in disguise.

When necessity leads us to use sincere words, the mask falls and we see the hypocritical man.

Anyone who tries to remedy the hatred of the eyes with a smile on their lips acts with hypocrisy.

In people with limited abilities, modesty is simple honesty, but in those with great talent it is hypocrisy.

How To Deal With False People

Is there a friend or family member who suddenly acts as if "you don't know his true nature"? Have you been harassed or threatened by someone pretending to have another personality? You're not the only one. Fake people are everywhere and are usually in dire need of attention. Fortunately, with a few simple steps you can get rid of the negative influence exerted by braggart, envious and hypocritical.

1

Avoid the hypocrite. Whenever you are dealing with a person who irritates or treats you badly, the best move is almost always the simplest: avoid those who exasperate you. Attend her as little as possible. The less you frequent it, the less opportunity it has to make you nervous.

- The most interesting side of this attitude is that it will turn into a subtle punishment for those who act hypocritically. If he continues to behave this way he will not have the privilege of being in your company

2

If you can't avoid her, interact with her as little as possible. It's not hard to decide who to hang out with. However, in certain circumstances you can't help but relate to fake people (for example, in group events). In these cases, avoid being rude by completely ignoring them. Conversely, try to behave politely without being overly likeable, which will decrease the risk of having a conversation with them.

- A good rule of thumb is to avoid talking to these types of people until they take the initiative or until you have a good reason for doing so. Be nice, but keep your distance, kind of like talking to someone you don't know.

3

Don't be bothered by hypocrisy. It is very important to remain calm when in contact with fake people, especially if they are very irritating.

- It is almost always better to walk away from an unfortunate situation than to lose patience with someone who gets on your nerves because of their lack of sincerity. Don't hesitate to give yourself a few minutes to calm down if you are about to explode.

- However, if he disrespects you, don't react the same way and don't lose control. False people need to realize that there are limits to their behavior, so respond politely by saying, "I don't accept that you talk to me like this."

- 4

- Don't stoop to their level. Don't be hypocritical if you're trying to fight certain people's falsehoods. Resist the temptation to "reciprocate with the same coin" by fueling petty gossip or making misconceptions. Remember that if you behave this way, others won't be able to tell the difference between your behavior and what you object to..

How to Handle a Fake Friend

1

Face the situation head on. One thing is a classmate or an acquaintance having a superficial behavior, another is when a close friend starts pretending. Since you cannot avoid or ignore him very easily, there is a risk that his behavior will negatively interfere with your life. If you suddenly notice a change in his behavior that doesn't look anything like his usual behavior, tell him about it. However, be prepared for his objections. Nobody likes to feel criticized.

• For example, if you notice that you hang out with hateful and insignificant people to give yourself importance, don't hide your bewilderment. Be polite, but don't be afraid to tell him that you think his choice is disastrous.

2

Ask a few questions to understand what his hypocrisy depends on. If you understand "why" he behaves this way, you will have less trouble understanding his transgressions. By asking him about his new attitude, you will be able to understand what is going on, but be careful not to disrespect him. Don't treat it badly if you can avoid it. For example, try asking him:

• "You know, I've noticed you've been acting differently lately. What's going on?";

• "So you're dating other people, huh?";

• "Where did this news you talk about lately come from?".

3

Consider addressing the problem directly if it is severe. In a way, a friend's choices are only about him. However, if the desire to pretend to be different leads him to do unwise things, as a friend don't wait to intervene. You probably won't be able to stop him, but you can let him know he's hurting himself.

• If you get carried away in situations that endanger your health (such as drug use), consult a psychologist or your parents. Sure they will get angry, but this is the best solution.

- Only take this initiative if you are truly concerned about their safety. It is not your job to control his choices.

4

Talk to your friends about the problem. Keep in mind that you don't have to fight the lie alone. If you have noticed that a friend has changed their attitude, it is very likely that others have also noticed. When he's not around, discuss the situation together. They may have a different point of view or provide information that simplifies the interpretation of the whole story. You can all decide together how to handle this person's new behavior.

- Prevent the issue from turning into a "state affair". Remember that your goal is to talk about the changes your friend has made in their way of doing things. This is not an excuse to deceive him or make recriminations about him.

- 5

- Be willing to temporarily distance yourself. In the end, you can't force anyone to stop pretending. If you have trouble getting your eyes open, take a step back. Let the whole situation resolve itself before resuming appointments. Avoid going out alone with him and limit your interactions when you are at a party. By showing him that his fake ways keep you from relating to him, you may be able to convince him to quit. If not, at least limit the occasions when it might bother you.

It is not easy to lose a friend because of their falsehood. However much you may suffer, don't let this problem ruin your life. If it exasperates you, take some time for yourself. Put your happiness first.

Another solution is to treat fake people the same way they treat you. It's not guaranteed to work, but it can sometimes prove that their behavior hurts you.

How to defend yourself from bad people: but why are some like this?

The issue of evil in the world is one of the most debated in humanity and we certainly did not deal with it first. Nor can we talk too much about it. Or try to solve it here right now on two feet or on four if we count yours and mine.

It is well established that evil and wickedness are inherent in the human being. Because? Probably because aggression, force and even violence are functional to survival, especially in a hostile environment in which individuals and species have to fight for life.

So it is obvious that man at the biological level is "built" to contain the "evil" in himself and that therefore also natural selection has done its job.

To this is added that on an aggressive and selfish nature for biological, functional reasons, culture overlaps, with rules, prohibitions, prejudices, superstructures, beliefs and mental structures, often very dysfunctional, and that's it.

The aggressiveness and selfishness necessary for the conservation of the individual and the species are masked and transformed into our daily evil, the one we more or less consciously suffer and more or less consciously inflict and the one we learn through the different channels of information, not least the history books, cinema and literature.

Because evil, like love, is a narrative theme with an unbeatable force.

If there is not so much bad in a good story, a lot of love (better if suffered) and a little good, it can't be a good story.

It is the irresistible fascination of wickedness and evil. Like that of the assholes, anyway.

Let's not forget that, apart from the natural resources of aggression fundamental to life on the planet, outside the jungle, the savannah and the caves, the bad guys, according to my theory (and not just mine), are bad because they have some problems. of personal balance and inner serenity.

This is not out of compassion or to justify them or even as a "consolation prize". As if to say: "Ebbé, oh, he's an asshole, but he's having a bad time, let's console ourselves and so on."

It is useful to know that when we are dealing with a bad person very often we are dealing with a person who is not at all happy.

This can help us treat it effectively. That's all, without so many fancy flights.

This is why it is important to know how to defend yourself against bad people.

How to defend yourself from bad people: what is useful to do

To defend oneself from bad people, in the meantime, one must know how to recognize evil and keep oneself in the healthy and beneficial balance between paranoia (that is, always seeing everything and everyone focused on us and against us), victimization and mania for persecution and gullibility, naivety, underestimation.

Bad people, that is, that large group, within which there are also men who abuse and manipulate, assholes and bastards, etc., want to control others to achieve their personal goals. Often very clear and obvious goals, often quite confused (when there is dysfunction and stupidity together).

Evil, we said, is democratic: sooner or later everyone - even the worst - we suffer it or we find someone who wants to inflict it on us and sooner or later we all "act" on others.

Let's say that the real villain is characterized by the constancy, quality and quantity of his own badness. And for motives and motivations.

Evil and cruel people can be found on all levels: from the African dictator to the ecological operator of Bournemouth.

No longer living in savannas and jungles, the average modern man shows his wickedness above all in the workplace - and for business reasons - in the family or in an apartment building or in court, or on Facebook (mom, what wretches! wicked, alas. Most pernicious.).

The casuistry of types of human slime is wider than the universe, which is infinite.

The bad guys are not always democratic, that is, not everyone is democratic. Some are bad with the good and the bad, others only with the good.

Keep this in mind when you are too good, as (your) goodness can often hurt you.

It is necessary - also to avoid unnecessary waste of energy - to be able to distinguish who is "only" stupid, rude and ignorant from who is bad or even bad as well as stupid, rude and ignorant.

Effective attitudes for dealing with bad people

I said above that one must be able to recognize the wickedness, that is, the abuse, invasion, violence of others.

It seems impossible, but most of us do not know how to defend ourselves from bad people and above all do not know how to recognize abuse.

In particular, a civic culture of respect for others and awareness of abuse is often totally lacking.

Because if people don't know how to recognize abuse, they can be abused better than them. It is clear to you, right?

Abuse occurs whenever a person is treated not as a person, but as a means, as a tool to achieve goals. Even emotional.

They abuse you, so they are bad, all people who want to have your body, have your time and have your money only for their own benefit, without giving you an advantage or worrying about an advantage for you and without considering your good and / or even aiming to harm you.

Anyone can be mean to you - even your parents and your brothers and sisters. Your sons.

Abuse of you who knows your weaknesses and gives you emotional low blows, for the sake of hurting you emotionally or for what has been said before, that is to convince you to give your body, your time and your money (or your personal resources and materials) without giving you a real advantage in proportion, without considering your own good or with the intention of harming you. Just so as not to repeat the important concepts.

If you think about it under this umbrella there are all the abusive behaviors you can imagine.

Those of two-person relationships, those of family and parent-child relationships, those of work relationships, including exploitation, blackmail and bullying.

There is also financial abuse, which is very common in couples and families.

How to defend yourself from bad people then?

If you have known me a little, you will also know my theory that toxic, negative and bad people are to be avoided and that our lifestyle, our habits and our choices must definitely go in that direction, for the duration of the our existence.

So you have to physically and emotionally distance yourself from toxic people and environments.

Then it is important to let go of one's naivety, abandon it, forget it, transform from naive children into adult, shrewd, cunning people.

This allows you to know and recognize your own value, to show it without hesitation and at the same time with discretion to others, to be respected and to recognize the wickedness and intentions of others.

"Si vis pacem, para bellum" the Romans said, meaning that if you want peace you must be ready for war. Being ready for war (an immortal rule still followed to keep balance in the world) means being armed and not helpless, without tools.

Being prudent, aware of one's value and enforcing one's borders means being ready for war, aspiring to peace.

The bad guys are dissuaded from those with tools.

Of course, it is not a good life, but sometimes it is necessary.

Make it clear from the outset in an implicit but clear way that your body, your money and your time have a price, in the higher end of the market.

Or, even, like credit card advertising, "they are priceless".

In addition, I recommend that you stick to these 3 basic rules.

Bad guys are NOT to be treated well. Everyone must be treated with respect, education and courtesy. But there are people (the bad guys) who understand only one language, what they speak. That of violence and malice. It is not necessary to be bad and violent (eh, no, otherwise what game are we playing?), But essential, determined, strong and courageous. Bread with bread and wine with wine. Few coaxing and ban on chattering with bad guys. Even if they are chased by hordes of toadies, it is not necessary to stand in the queue. Your dignity is the boundary that scares even the bad guys. Keep in mind that with bad guys, you must especially avoid being empathetic. Bad? Empathy, go away!

2. Don't fall into the traps that the bad guys set: Bad people know your weaknesses far better than you do and set pitfalls that make you lose control over you and take it from them. For example, they know perfectly well what makes you angry and in the workplace and in the family they make you angry as they please to get you in trouble and in the minority. Don't fall for it. Get to know yourself and your weaknesses better than anyone else, so you can protect yourself.

3. Get a life. Also make a plan B. Always. For anything. If we are in a state of frailty alone, we are more vulnerable to wickedness than bad people. It is typical, for example, in cases of mobbing, i.e. psychological violence in the workplace, that people are targeted

who are already in difficulty due to economic problems or in their family or in their relationship or who are very attached to their job of work. Totally dedicated and with nothing else out there. You have a "full" life, complete, full of interests, so in cases like these, waiting to leave and leave the toxic environment, you can recharge yourself out of the toxic situation or, even better, less likely to become a target of bad people. For this, in the same way, we must not give all of ourselves to the couple relationship and family life, but to have a job or a chance to work.

Four types of fake people that are easy to spot in everyday life

"Of course Dude is really fake", "Mmm, I don't trust you, she's a fake person", "Sounds friendly, but he's fake."

It is rather curious to attribute to a person the quality of "fake". A person is not a statement that may or may not be true. But there can be a disconnect between inside and outside, between his actions and his thoughts, a kind of inconsistency that covers deep and authentic intentions with poses, fictions, artifices.

You quickly understand that the concept is gigantic, and can include both who you thought was your friend and stabbed you in the back for money, and the nephew telling you not to worry because he loves hot pasta, and the boyfriend who cheats on you in secret, and who gives you a hole in giving yourself sick at the last minute. The profile of the lie is changing, embracing good and evil, many different actions with different motives. So it is wise not to give this term to people: because as suggestive as it is, it is too generic, and does not allow you to choose without equivocation a nuance between Judas and kindness. Much better to try to understand what kind of fake it is and choose the most exact word. We see four species: actually there would be dozens of them to observe, but these are among the main branches.

Hypocritical

In Greek, hypokrités is the actor. Thus the hypocrite has a part in real life: from scene to scene he pretends, he shows himself different from what he is intimately, from what he really believes and wants.

The acquaintance who welcomes us with great warmth but then speaks ill of us behind our back is a hypocrite; the politician who fights an alleged battle of civilization out of mere self-interest is hypocritical; we are hypocrites when we blatantly criticize those who do not do the separate collection well and then throw the butts on the ground.

They are probably the most common cases of fakes and have many types, such as traitors, bigots and simulators.

Liar

This is more specific and describes that fake who chooses the vehicle of words. A smile may be enough to be hypocritical, but to be a liar you need language, you need a false proposition: it brings us close to the false logic. A liar can be someone who lies about where he was last night, a liar is the child who clears himself with an imaginative reconstruction of the facts, a liar who tells us a lie about why he wasn't there in time of need. Around the liar we often find the deceiver.

False

Often the fiction of the fake aims to show a substance that is not there. If the acting of the actor is fiction, even the scenography, the costume are fiction - and such is the false. An inconsistent fake, even illegitimate. False career or vaunted nobility to be put on display, fake wealth flaunted to please and be admired, fake interest shown only to circumvent. Brother of the illusory and of the artifact.

Courteous

In courtesy, in kindness, there is always a screen component, of flattering fiction. There is hypocrisy in appreciating a poorly cooked dish, there is a lie in "Thank you, you shouldn't have!", There is a fake in the salutation formulas. They are not only harmless but also civil lies. And just to account for the goodness of the fake that is courteous, kind, polite, it is good to specify our judgments.

In short, the next time we hear about a 'false person' let's ask ourselves: false in what sense? And we respond with a word

Conclusion:

I hope that these reflections that I have tried to do with you have helped you to see the dynamics of relationships from a different perspective.

I hope that this book, with some well-known theories, some less so, may have helped you to cultivate your temperament, exercise your will and enlighten your heart and soul in order to make choices in total freedom and awareness.

I hope that this book, which tries to deal in a synthetic and direct way with the problems of manipulation in today's world, has shown you what Dark Psychology & Manipulation is and suggested possible defense solutions.

I hope the narration was enjoyable, full of ideas and questions.

If I managed to get your attention even for a few moments, I'm happy.

Thank you very much dear reader and listener. If you are satisfied and intrigued, you can continue the journey by reading the other books that follow in this series.

Thanks thanks thanks !!!

I wish you a good life!

See you soon.

And remember:

The most difficult and exhausting of all vices, hypocrisy is a round-the-clock task.